THE SATURDAY EVENING POST

I Can Cook...
Children's Cookbook

THE SATURDAY EVENING POST

I Can Cook...
Children's Cookbook

Color Me

The Curtis Publishing Company
Indianapolis, Indiana

The editors wish to extend
a special note of thanks to
Julie Nixon Eisenhower for
compiling these recipes—
many of which are from
her personal files.

Book designed and illustrated by
Don Moldroski

Now You, Too, Can Cook!

All you need to get started are easy-to-follow recipes like these, a little imagination, a willingness to clean up a few spills or dirty pots and pans and the occasional supervision of Mom or Dad.

In fact, it's a good idea to let Mom and Dad know that you are about to experiment in the kitchen so that they can be on hand to help if needed (and to sample your tasty morsels, as well!)

Of course, while you are being creative in the kitchen, you will also want to be careful. The following tips can help you become a safety-conscious cook:

When pulling out a plug, always grasp the plug, not the cord.

Keep your hands dry while working in the kitchen. Wet, slippery hands can cause spills and accidents. They are also hazardous when working with electrical appliances.

Keep your pot holders dry. A wet pot holder absorbs heat and can lead to burns.

When cutting with a knife, always cut away from yourself.

Remember to tip the lid away from you whenever you raise the cover of a hot pan. This helps prevent steam burns.

Never leave the handle of a pan extended over the edge of the range or counter. Someone might bump it and cause a spill.

And, while you're being careful, remember to enjoy yourself! An eager cook like you—together with a book like this—can't miss. You *can* do it!

The Editors

Cooking Terms to Help You Along the Way

Bake — Cook in oven.

Beat — Mix very fast with a spoon or fork, or round and round with a rotary beater.

Blend — Mix 2 or more ingredients until smooth.

Boil — Cook until liquid is so hot it bubbles.

Broil — Cook directly under heating unit in range, or over hot coals.

Chop — Cut into pieces with a knife or chopper.

Cream — Beat until fluffy and creamy.

Cube — Cut into ¼- to ½-inch squares.

Dot — Drop bits of butter or cheese over the entire surface of the food you are cooking.

Drain — Pour off liquid.

Grate — Rub cheese, carrots, etc. against grater to cut into small flakelike pieces. Be sure to have an adult help you when using the grater.

Grease — Spread bottom and sides of pan with shortening.

Knead — Work with your hands.

Melt — Heat until liquid.

Mince — Chop or cut into tiny pieces.

Mound — Heap food into a mountain shape.

Peel — Pull off outer skin, as from an orange or banana.

Sift — Put through flour sifter or fine sieve.

Simmer — Cook over very low heat until liquid is hot but not bubbling.

Stir — Mix round and round with spoon.

Toss — Mix ingredients lightly.

Whip — Beat with rotary egg beater or electric mixer to add air.

Table of Contents

Good Morning Breakfasts

Doughnut Surprise

serves 4

4 plain doughnuts
8 teaspoons butter
8 teaspoons honey
8 teaspoons shredded coconut

Slice doughnuts sideways.

•

Whip the butter and honey together and spread on each half.
Sprinkle each with 1 teaspoon coconut.

•

Toast under broiler at 350 degrees for about 5 minutes.

Gold in the Mountain

A fun and different way to begin the day.
serves 1

1 cup yogurt
1/2 cup of your favorite fruit
1 tablespoon toasted wheat germ

In a cereal bowl, make a mountain of yogurt. Hide pieces of
your favorite fruit inside the mountain — cherries,
pineapple, peaches, grapes, bananas, melon.

•

Sprinkle wheat germ on top.

Goldilocks' Porridge

serves 4

3 cups water
1 cup dried apricots
1 1/3 cups Instant Quaker Oats
Cinnamon
Honey
Cream or milk

Bring water to a boil and add apricots.
Cook for 5 minutes over low heat.

•

Add oatmeal to boiling water with fruit
and cook for 1 minute.

•

Cover pan and remove from heat.

•

After 3 minutes, spoon into cereal bowls and top
with cinnamon, honey and cream or milk.

Cheddar Muffin Breakfast

serves 4

4 cornbread muffins
8 slices cheddar cheese

Slice muffins in half crosswise.

•

Top each muffin half with a thin slice of cheese and
place under broiler until cheese melts.

Get-Up-and-Go Orange Drink

serves 2

1 egg
1/2 cup milk
1 (6-ounce) can frozen orange juice

Place all ingredients in blender and whip until smooth.

Ham and Eggs

serves 4

1 (4 1/2-ounce) can deviled ham
8 soda crackers, crushed
4 eggs

Mix deviled ham with cracker crumbs. Place 2 tablespoons in each of 4 muffin tins. Pat some of the ham partially up the sides of the tins.

•

Drop eggs on top of ham.

•

Cut piece of aluminum foil a little larger than the muffin pan. Cut small hole in center to allow the steam to escape. Place aluminum foil loosely over eggs so they will stay tender while baking.

•

Bake in 325-degree preheated oven until eggs are firm — about 15 minutes.

•

To serve, scoop ham and eggs out of muffin pans onto 4 slices of buttered toast.

Quick and Cool Breakfast

A breakfast which takes one minute to make.
serves 2

1 ripe cantaloupe
1 cup plain yogurt
2 cherries

Cut melon in half and remove seeds.
●
Fill center of each half melon with ½ cup yogurt.
●
Top with cherry.

Banana Shake

A favorite snack for any time of day.
serves 1

1 ripe banana
1 teaspoon vanilla
1 cup plain yogurt

Place all ingredients in blender for one minute.
●
Pour into tall glass and serve.

Banana in a Blanket

serves 4

4 bananas, peeled
4 thin slices boiled ham
4 teaspoons margarine

Wrap each banana with ham slice, top with margarine
and place in baking dish.

●

Bake 8 minutes at 425 degrees, or until ham is light brown.

French Toast

serves 2

2 eggs
2 tablespoons wheat germ
2 tablespoons water
1 teaspoon vanilla
1 teaspoon honey
2 tablespoons oil
4 pieces cracked wheat bread

In small bowl beat eggs; then stir in wheat germ.
water, vanilla and honey.

●

Heat oil in skillet over medium heat.

●

Dip each bread slice into egg mixture.

●

Place in frying pan and cook until bread is
brown on both sides.

●

Serve with butter and syrup.

Salads

St. Patrick's Day Shamrock Pears

*But these beautiful green pears with a mint flavor are
good any time of the year.*
serves 4

1 jar mint jelly
2 drops green food coloring
4 canned pear halves
4 lettuce leaves
4 scoops cottage cheese

Put jelly in saucepan and stir over low heat
until jelly melts. Stir in food coloring.

Dip each pear half in jelly, coating it green.

Place pear half on lettuce leaf and fill center
with cottage cheese.

Apple Salad

serves 2

1 apple, sliced
1 celery stalk, sliced
2 tablespoons mayonnaise
2 tablespoons Swiss cheese, shredded
1 tablespoon walnuts, chopped

In a bowl, mix all the ingredients together.

Serve on lettuce leaves.

Easy Four-Bean Salad

A wonderful salad which keeps in the refrigerator for days.
serves 4 to 6

1 (1-pound) can red kidney beans
1 (1-pound) can lima beans
1 (1-pound) can wax beans
1 (1-pound) can French-cut green beans
1 large onion
1/2 cup honey
1/2 cup oil
1/2 cup cider vinegar
1/2 teaspoon pepper

Drain and rinse kidney beans.
Drain lima, wax and green beans.

•

Mix the four kinds of beans.

•

Slice onion, separate slices into rings
and add to bean mixture.

•

Combine honey, oil, vinegar and pepper.

•

Pour over bean-onion mixture and toss.

•

Refrigerate several hours or overnight.

Bananas in the Jungle

It's fun to look for the bananas in the green jungle.
serves 4

1/2 **head lettuce**
10 fresh spinach leaves
1 ripe banana
4 tablespoons Russian dressing

Wash lettuce and spinach leaves;
tear into bite-size pieces.

Pat leaves dry with paper towels.

Slice banana into the salad and toss with your
favorite Russian dressing.

Five Cup Salad

This one's great for hot, sunny summer days.
serves 6

1 cup mandarin oranges, drained
1 cup chunk pineapple, drained
1 cup chopped walnuts
1 cup coconut
1 cup sour cream, yogurt or whipped cream

Mix all ingredients together and let stand in
refrigerator overnight.

Add 1 cup drained fruit cocktail for variety.

Out-of-this-World Chicken Salad

serves 6

2 (11-ounce) cans mandarin oranges, drained
1/4 cup chopped almonds
1 banana, sliced
2 cups chicken cut into cubes
1/2 pound sharp cheddar cheese, cubed
1/2 cup mayonnaise
12 pineapple rings

Mix oranges, almonds, banana slices, chicken, cheese
and mayonnaise in a bowl.

•

Place 2 pineapple rings on each plate.

•

Mound chicken salad on top of pineapple
rings and serve.

Skinny Salad Dressing

A low-calorie dressing everyone will like.
serves 4

1 cup plain low-fat yogurt
1 teaspoon honey
2 teaspoons lemon juice

Mix well. Serve over fruit salad.

Before-You-Go-To-Bed Cucumbers

These cucumbers taste best when they spend the night in the refrigerator.
They are so good you'll want them for
breakfast, lunch and dinner.
serves 4 to 6

4 peeled and sliced cucumbers
1 cup Wishbone Italian salad dressing
3 tablespoons white vinegar
1 teaspoon pepper
1/4 cup honey

Slice cucumbers into rounds.

Stir dressing, vinegar and pepper into the honey
and pour over cucumbers.

Place in refrigerator before you go to bed.

Next day serve on bed of lettuce.

Three "P" Salad

serves 4

1 (14 1/2-ounce) can peas
1 cup Spanish peanuts
1 cup diced sweet pickles
1/3 cup mayonnaise

Drain peas and mix with the remaining ingredients.

At its crunchy best when served fresh.

Soups

Snowflake Soup

This snow can fall on any soup.
serves 3

1 can potato soup
1 soup can milk
1/2 cup popped corn
3 tablespoons grated Swiss cheese

Mix soup and milk in saucepan and stir until hot.

•

Pour soup into bowls.

•

Float popcorn (snow) and shredded cheese
on top of each bowl of soup.

Count-to-Ten Egg Drop Soup

It's fun to watch the egg turn into ribbons
as you count to ten.
serves 4

2 (10-ounce) cans chicken broth
2 soup cans of water
2 eggs
2 teaspoons soy sauce or tamari

Place soup and water in saucepan and heat to boiling.

•

In small bowl, beat eggs and soy sauce (with rotary beater).

•

Pour eggs into hot broth and stir while you count to 10.

•

Serve immediately.

One-Two-Three Soup

Just three cans to open for a quick, delicious soup.
serves 4

1 can tomato soup
1 can green pea soup
1 can beef consomme
1 teaspoon chopped chives, if desired

Empty all three cans into saucepan.

•

Heat until hot, stirring constantly.

•

Sprinkle with chopped chives before serving.

Pink Panther Soup

You will want to eat this soup every day of the week.
serves 6

2 (l-pound) cans tomatoes
Juice of one lemon
1/4 teaspoon basil
1/4 teaspoon curry powder
16 ounces plain yogurt

Drain tomatoes.

•

Place all ingredients in blender and blend until smooth.

•

Put blender in refrigerator for at least 1 hour before serving.

Blushing Corn Chowder

serves 2

1 can tomato soup
1 soup can of milk
1 teaspoon honey
1/2 cup cream-style corn

Empty soup and milk into saucepan.

•

Stir in honey and corn.

•

Heat until hot; do not boil.

•

Serve immediately.

"You Better Eat Your Spinach, Soupy"

You and your friends will love this combination!
serves 2

1 can chicken or turkey soup
1/2 cup cooked spinach

Heat soup and spinach together and serve.

Sandwiches

Skyhigh Sandwich

When you make this sandwich, let your imagination run wild.
serves 1

Bun or brown bread
2 tablespoons Russian dressing
2 tablespoons pickle relish
2 slices bologna
1 hard-cooked egg, sliced
Lettuce, tomato slice, green pepper
1 slice your favorite cheese
2 slices turkey
2 slices bacon

Spread bread with Russian dressing and pickle relish
and stack all other ingredients on top.
•

Finish with other slice of bread or bun.

Soup Sandwich

For cold days when you can't decide between
soup or a sandwich.
serves 6

1 can tomato soup
1 cup shredded or cubed cheddar cheese
6 pieces whole wheat toast

Place tomato soup in saucepan.
•

Add cheese and cook until cheese melts.
•

Pour over toasted bread.

Crabby but Good

When you feel like mixing lots of ingredients together.
serves 4

1 (8-ounce) package cream cheese
1 (6-ounce) can crab meat, drained
1 teaspoon Worcestershire sauce
1 teaspoon instant onion
1 tablespoon lemon juice
4 English muffins
8 slices cheese
2 tomatoes, each cut in 4 slices

Mix cream cheese, crab, Worcestershire sauce,
instant onion and lemon juice.

•

Spread mixture on muffin halves.

•

Place 1 cheese and tomato slice on each muffin.

•

Bake at 350 degrees for 15 minutes.

Color Me

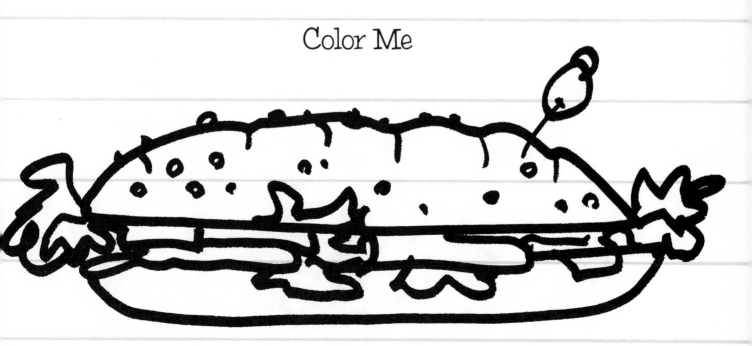

Peanut Pumpernickel Sandwich

If you can say it, you can make — and eat it.
serves 1

2 slices pumpernickel bread
Mayonnaise
Lettuce leaf
2 slices crisp bacon
4 tablespoons peanut butter

Spread 1 slice of bread with mayonnaise.

Place lettuce leaf and bacon slices on top.

Spread other slice with peanut butter.

Join halves for peanut pumpernickel sandwich.

Color Me

4-4-4 Crab Muffins

*When you want to surprise your mother with a
quick and different tasting lunch.*
serves 2

1 English muffin
4 tablespoons cream cheese
4 tablespoons crab meat, canned
4 tablespoons cocktail sauce

Cut muffin in half and toast.

•

Spread each half with 2 tablespoons cream cheese.

•

Place 2 tablespoons crab on each muffin
and top with cocktail sauce.

Thousand Island Tuna

serves 4

1 small can tuna fish, drained
1/3 cup Thousand Island dressing
1/4 cup peanuts, chopped
1 egg, chopped

Mix all ingredients together and spread
on toasted bread.

•

Place lettuce leaf in each sandwich if desired.

Dog on a Stick

serves 4

4 hot dogs
4 slices bacon
1 (8-ounce) can pineapple chunks
4 skewers

Cut each hot dog and bacon slice into 3 pieces.

•

Thread onto each skewer a hot dog piece,
pineapple chunk and bacon slice.

•

Place the skewers on cookie sheet and broil
for 5 minutes on each side.

Devil Sandwich

serves 4

1 (4 1/2-ounce) can deviled ham
2 hard-cooked eggs, chopped
1 teaspoon horseradish
2 tablespoons diced sweet pickle
1 tablespoon milk

Blend until smooth.

•

Spread on your favorite bread.

•

Raisin bread is especially good with this.

Beef

Kima

A Pakistani dish with the flavor of the Orient
serves 4 to 6

1 cup chopped onions
3 tablespoons butter
1 pound ground beef
1/4 teaspoon garlic powder
1 tablespoon curry powder
3 teaspoons soy sauce or tamari
Dash pepper
2 tomatoes, cut up
2 potatoes, cut in very small pieces
1 (10-ounce) package frozen peas
1 (10 1/2-ounce) can pineapple chunks, drained
Shredded coconut

Cook onion in butter over low heat until golden.
Add meat and stir over low heat until lightly browned.

•

Add the next 7 ingredients.

•

Cover and simmer for 25 minutes.

•

Stir in pineapple and sprinkle with shredded coconut before serving.

Beef Casserole in a Pan

serves 6

1 1/2 pounds ground beef
2 tablespoons minced onions
1 (11-ounce) can condensed cheddar cheese soup
1 (8 3/4-ounce) can whole-kernel corn, drained
1 (4 1/2-ounce) can sliced mushrooms, drained
1 teaspoon garlic powder
1/2 teaspoon honey

Brown beef in large frying pan over medium heat.

Stir in minced onions.

Add all other ingredients and heat until boiling.

Cook over very low heat for 15 minutes.

Hamburger Goulash

serves 4

1 1/2 pounds hamburger
1/8 cup vegetable oil
1 green pepper, chopped
1 (1-pound) can tomatoes
1 (1-pound) can green beans
2 tablespoons minced onions

In vegetable oil, cook hamburger until meat loses its pink color.

Stir in green pepper, tomatoes, green beans and minced onions.

Cook 15 minutes over low heat. Serve over rice or noodles.

Daddy's Favorite Steak

You'll enjoy making this steak and sauce because
everyone loves to eat it. Surprise your father
with this special dinner.
serves 4

4 small steaks (filet mignon, rib eye, etc.)
Coarsely ground pepper or Lawry's seasoned pepper
1/2 stick butter
1/4 cup beef broth
2/3 cup heavy cream
1/2 teaspoon thyme
4 slices bacon, fried and crumbled

Press lots of pepper into both sides of the steak.

•

Heat heavy iron skillet; add butter.

•

When butter is melted, brown meat over medium heat
(5 minutes on each side).

•

Remove steaks.

•

Turn heat to low and add beef broth to frying pan; stir well.

•

Simmer for a minute.

•

Add cream and thyme and let simmer on low heat for a few
minutes. Lastly, add crumbled bacon.

•

Spoon sauce over steak (and rice, noodles or potato)
and serve.

Five Hour Stew

*Make this in the morning and smell the delicious
stew aroma all day.*
serves 6

2 pounds of beef stew meat
3 medium onions, chopped
1 cup celery, chopped
6 carrots, chopped
2 cups tomato juice
1 slice bread (broken up)
3 tablespoons tapioca
1 tablespoon honey
1 1/2 teaspoons garlic powder
1/2 teaspoon pepper
4 potatoes, quartered

Mix all ingredients together and bake in a covered dish
for 5 hours at 250 degrees.

Fancy Dinner Hamburger

serves 6

2 pounds ground beef
1 package Lipton's onion soup mix
1 teaspoon Worcestershire sauce
1 teaspoon soy sauce or tamari
1 teaspoon lemon juice

Mix all ingredients.

Shape meat into patties and broil 5 minutes on each side.

Spaghetti Meat Sauce

*A favorite dinner recipe because it is easy and delicious —
and you can't fail.*
serves 4

1/8 **cup salad oil**
1 1/2 **pounds hamburger**
2 **cups tomato juice**
2 **small cans tomato paste**
2 **tablespoons minced onion**
1 **teaspoon garlic powder**
1 **teaspoon pepper**
1 **teaspoon chili powder**
1 **teaspoon honey**

Brown meat in salad oil.

•

Stir in juice, tomato paste, onions, garlic, pepper,
chili powder and honey.

•

Cook over very low heat for 45 minutes.

Color Me

Spicy Beef Cakes

serves 4 to 6

1 1/2 pounds ground round
1 egg
1/2 cup bottled barbecue sauce
1/2 teaspoon chili powder

In bowl mix beef, egg, barbecue sauce and chili powder.

Spoon mixture into 6 large muffin pan cups or 6-ounce custard cups.

Bake at 350 degrees for 40 minutes.

Spaghetti Meat Loaf

serves 6

1 1/2 pounds ground beef
1 (1-pound) can spaghetti in tomato sauce
1 egg
1/8 teaspoon garlic powder
4 slices American cheese
2 tablespoons minced onion

Gently mix ground beef with spaghetti, egg and garlic powder.

Press half the mixture into an 8-by-8-by-2-inch baking pan.

Top with cheese slices and minced onion.

Then spoon remaining beef mixture over all to form loaf.

Bake at 350 degrees for 1 hour.

Six Layer Dinner

serves 4

4 potatoes, sliced
3 onions, sliced
1 (number 2 1/2) can tomatoes, drained
1 pound hamburger
1/2 cup uncooked rice
4 slices raw bacon

In a large casserole, place potato slices;
next onion slices and tomatoes.

•

Spread the hamburger on top of the tomatoes.

•

Sprinkle rice over all and lay bacon on top.

Add cold water to the casserole dish until it reaches
the top of the ingredients.

•

Cover and bake for 2 hours at 350 degrees.

Chicken

Golden Chicken

serves 4

6 chicken legs (about 2 1/2 pounds)
2 tablespoons melted butter
1 can golden mushroom soup
1/4 cup grape juice
1/8 teaspoon nutmeg
1/4 cup pimiento strips

In shallow baking dish, place chicken skin side up.

Pour melted butter over chicken.

Bake at 400 degrees for 40 minutes.

Combine remaining ingredients and spoon over chicken.

Bake 20 minutes more.

Deluxe Chicken Salad

serves 4

1 (5-ounce) can chicken
1/4 cup chopped walnuts
1/4 cup chopped almonds
2 teaspoons minced onion
2 teaspoons lemon juice
1/4 cup mayonnaise

Drain chicken well and flake with fork into a bowl.

Mix in the remaining ingredients and eat as is or
spread on your favorite bread.

Brown Paper Bag Chicken

Moist chicken every time — lots of finger licking!
serves 2 to 4

1 (2-pound) chicken, ready for roasting
Butter
Stuffing, if desired
1 brown paper bag

Rub entire chicken with butter.

●

After stuffing chicken (have your mother help you),
close leg and neck openings with string and toothpicks.

●

Place greased bird in brown paper bag.

●

Fold opening of bag under.

●

Place bag in shallow pan and roast at 400 degrees for 2 hours.

●

Split open bag and chicken is golden brown and ready to eat!

Color Me

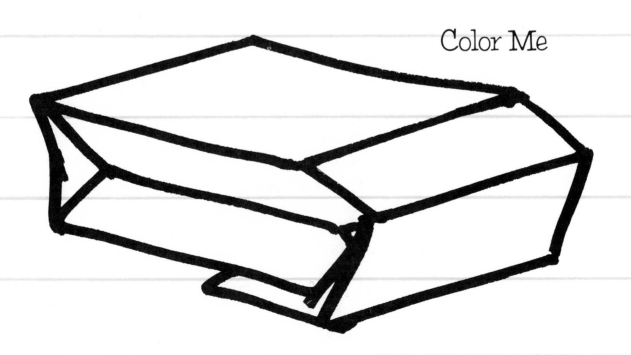

Very Easy Chicken-Rice Casserole

serves 4

1 can mushroom soup
1 can celery soup
1 soup can milk
1 cup uncooked rice
4 chicken breasts
1 package dry onion soup mix

Mix mushroom and celery soups, milk and rice
and pour into a greased casserole dish.

●

Place chicken on top of soup mixture
and sprinkle with onion soup.

●

Cover dish with aluminum foil and bake
at 325 degrees for 2 hours.

Peachy Chicken

serves 6

6 chicken breasts
1 bottle Russian dressing
1 (8-ounce) jar peach preserves
1 package dry onion soup mix

Place breasts in buttered pan.

●

Mix dressing, preserves and onion soup mix
and pour sauce over chicken. Cover.

●

Bake for 1 1/2 hours at 350 degrees.

Curry Coconut Chicken

serves 4

1 broiler-fryer, cut up (about 3 pounds)
1/2 stick butter
1/2 cup honey
1/4 cup prepared mustard
1 teaspoon curry powder
1/4 cup shredded coconut

Wash chicken pieces; pat dry.

Melt the butter in a shallow baking pan.

Stir in the remaining ingredients, except coconut.

Roll chicken in butter mixture to coat both sides.

Then arrange skin side up in a single layer in the same pan.

Bake at 375 degrees for 1 hour.

Sprinkle coconut on top before serving.

Color Me

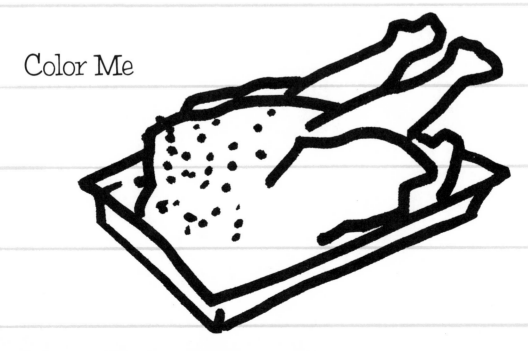

Honey Barbecued Chicken

serves 4

2 or 3 pounds chicken breasts and thighs
1 egg yolk
1/8 teaspoon pepper
1 teaspoon paprika
2 tablespoons soy sauce or tamari
1 tablespoon lemon juice
2 tablespoons melted butter
1/4 cup honey

Mix all ingredients except chicken together
and dip chicken pieces in sauce.

•

Lay chicken in pan.

•

Pour rest of sauce over all.

•

Bake for 30 minutes at 400 degrees; turn chicken
pieces over and bake for another 40 minutes.

Seafood

Night-Before Crab Casserole

*Before you go to bed make this delicious dinner
and enjoy it the next night!*
serves 6

3 slices bread
2 (6-ounce) cans crab meat, drained
1 cup mayonnaise
1 cup half-and-half
6 hard-cooked eggs, chopped
1 tablespoon minced onion
1/2 cup cornflake crumbs

Take crusts off bread and cut into cubes.

•

Mix crab, mayonnaise, half-and-half, eggs, onion
and bread cubes.

•

Place in greased casserole dish and put in
refrigerator overnight.

•

An hour before dinner, sprinkle cornflake crumbs over top
and bake at 350 degrees for 1 hour.

Color Me

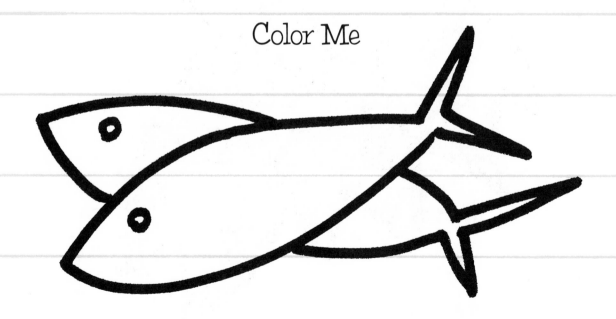

Sole

serves 4

1 1/2 pounds frozen or fresh filet of sole
1 onion, sliced thin
1 cup sour cream
1 teaspoon paprika
1/2 cup grated Swiss cheese

Place sole (thawed) in greased baking dish.

Cover with onion slices.

Mix sour cream, paprika and cheese together
and pour over fish.

Bake at 375 degrees for 25 minutes.

Hurry Tuna

serves 4

1 can cream of mushroom soup
1/3 cup milk
1 (7-ounce) can tuna, drained
2 hard-cooked eggs, quartered
4 buttered toast slices
4 tablespoons grated Parmesan cheese

In a saucepan, stir over low heat soup, milk, tuna
and egg quarters

When hot, spoon mixture over buttered toast and top each
serving with a tablespoon of Parmesan cheese.

Delicious Shrimp Curry

This is very easy to make and more fun to eat!
serves 4

2 (3/4-pound) bags frozen shrimp
4 tablespoons butter
4 tablespoons flour
2 cups milk
6 tablespoons catsup
1 tablespoon curry powder
1 teaspoon paprika

Cook shrimp according to package directions and drain;
set aside.

•

Melt butter in saucepan over low heat.

•

Stir in flour until smooth.

•

Then stir in milk.

•

Add catsup, curry powder and paprika.

•

Cook over very low heat for 10 minutes,
stirring occasionally.

•

Lastly, stir in cooked shrimp and simmer 5 minutes more.

•

For a special touch, pass small bowls of 2 or 3 of the following:
chopped peanuts, chopped eggs, raisins, chutney,
chopped apple, or chopped onions.

Crab-Apple Quickie

serves 2

1 (6-ounce) can crab meat
1 apple, chopped
1 cup cooked rice
1/4 cup milk
1/4 cup mayonnaise
1/2 teaspoon curry powder

Mix all the above ingredients together and place
in small casserole dish.

•

Bake at 350 degrees for 15 minutes or until heated through.

Crispy Casserole

serves 4 to 6

1 (3/4-pound) can shrimp, drained
1 (1/2-pound) can crab, drained
1 cup mayonnaise
1 cup celery, chopped
1 onion, chopped
1 green pepper, chopped
1/2 cup toasted bread crumbs

Mix shrimp, crab, mayonnaise, celery, onion and green pepper.

•

Place in buttered casserole.

•

Sprinkle bread crumbs on top.

•

Bake at 350 degrees for 1/2 hour.

Fabulous Fish

Different and very good for a special party.
serves 4

1 (6-ounce) can crab meat, drained
1 (6-ounce) can small cocktail shrimp, drained
4 pieces filet of sole
1 (10-ounce) can cheddar cheese soup
4 slices lemon
Paprika

Mix crab meat and all but four of the shrimp.

•

Mound the seafood in the center of each piece
of sole and form roll.

•

Fasten the rolls with toothpicks holding 1 lemon slice
and a whole shrimp.

•

Place the rolls in a buttered casserole dish.

•

Pour soup over all and bake at 400 degrees for 25 minutes.

•

Sprinkle with paprika and serve.

Pork

Pork Chops
with Hawaiian Rice

*Make this one often, for "Hawaiian Rice" will soon
become one of your favorite foods.*
serves 4

4 lean loin pork chops
1/8 cup vegetable oil
1 cup water
1 cup uncooked rice
3/4 cup green pepper, chopped
1 (15-ounce) can tomato sauce with tidbits
1 (13-ounce) can pineapple chunks, undrained
1 tablespoon vinegar

Heat vegetable oil in large frying pan.

•

Add pork chops and brown on both sides.

•

In heavy saucepan, mix water, rice, green pepper, tomato sauce,
undrained pineapple chunks and vinegar.

•

Place chops on top of rice mixture.

•

Cook over low heat, tightly covered, for 1 hour.

Color Me

Corn Dogs

A different kind of hot dog.
serves 4

4 hot dogs
1/4 cup catsup
1/2 cup cornflake crumbs
1/4 cup grated cheddar cheese

Roll hot dogs in catsup, then cornflake crumbs.

•

Sprinkle each dog with grated cheese.

•

Bake for 15 minutes at 350 degrees.

Choppy Frankfurter Special

serves 4

4 large cooked frankfurters, sliced in 1/2-inch slices
2 hard-cooked eggs, chopped
1 tablespoon chili sauce
1 tablespoon sweet pickle relish
1 tablespoon chopped parsley
1 teaspoon sesame seeds
1 teaspoon prepared mustard
1/2 cup grated cheese

Combine all ingredients (except cheese) in a casserole.

•

Sprinkle top with cheese.

•

Bake in a preheated 350-degree oven for about 15 minutes.

Ham Quiche

Quiche is easy to prepare and it's so much fun to eat!
serves 4

4 eggs
2 cups lean ham, cooked and diced
8 ounces cottage cheese
1 tablespoon green pepper, chopped
1 teaspoon chives or onion, chopped
1/2 teaspoon dry mustard

Beat eggs lightly and stir in remaining ingredients.

•

Pour mixture into small greased casserole dish and bake in
preheated 350-degree oven for about 30 to 45 minutes,
or until set like a custard.

Milk-Baked Pork Chops

These pork chops are so tender, you can cut them with a fork.
serves 4

4 pork chops, 3/4-inch thick
4 teaspoons dry mustard
2 cups milk

Place chops in buttered baking dish.

•

Spread each chop with 1 teaspoon of dry mustard. Pour milk
into pan until it reaches top of the chops.

•

Bake uncovered at 350 degrees for 1 1/2 hours.

Dishes to go with Dinner

Brown Sugar Beans

serves 6

2 (1-pound) cans baked beans
4 slices bacon
1/2 cup dark brown sugar

Empty beans into baking dish.

•

Top beans with bacon slices.

•

Sprinkle sugar over all.

•

Cover and bake at 350 degrees for 30 minutes.

•

Uncover and continue baking for 30 minutes or until
bacon is done.

Oven "French Fries"

serves 4

4 unpeeled potatoes, washed
2 tablespoons vegetable oil
Paprika

Cut washed potatoes into 1/3-inch sticks (do not peel).

•

Toss sticks in salad bowl with vegetable oil.

•

Place potatoes on greased baking sheet. Sprinkle with paprika
and bake at 450 degrees for 8 minutes; then reduce heat
to 350 degrees and cook 10 minutes longer.

Honey Rice

serves 6

3 cups cooked rice
1/2 cup seedless raisins
2 1/2 cups milk
1/2 cup honey
2 tablespoons butter
1 teaspoon grated lemon peel
1 tablespoon lemon juice

Combine rice, raisins, milk, honey and butter in saucepan.

•

Stir in lemon peel and juice.

•

Bring to boil, reduce heat and cook over low heat uncovered
for 15 minutes, stirring occasionally.

Sweet, Sweet Potatoes

serves 6

1 (2 1/2-pound) can dry-pack sweet potatoes
1 stick butter
1 cup milk
1/2 teaspoon nutmeg
1/4 teaspoon cinnamon
3/4 cup honey

Mash potatoes with all other ingredients and place in casserole dish.

•

Bake at 325 degrees for 20 minutes, or until glazed on top.

Potato Smash

serves 4

3 cups cooked, sliced potatoes
1 cup cottage cheese
1/2 cup sour cream
1/2 cup chopped onions
1/2 cup grated Parmesan cheese

Stir potatoes, cottage cheese, sour cream and onions together.
Pour into buttered casserole.

•

Top with grated cheese. Bake at 350 degrees for 30 minutes.

Crusty Noodles

A wonderful and different treat with roast beef or lamb.
serves 6

1/2 pound thin noodles
1 tablespoon oil
1/2 stick butter

Cook noodles in water with oil; drain and rinse in cold water.

•

Melt butter in iron skillet.

•

When butter is sizzling hot, add noodles and
stir them around.

•

Reduce heat and cook very slowly until there is a
light brown crust on bottom of noodles.

Golden Potatoes

serves 4

2 (1-pound) cans small white potatoes
1/2 can cheddar cheese soup
1/2 can golden mushroom soup
1 soup can of milk
1/8 teaspoon garlic powder

Drain potatoes.

Place in greased baking dish.

Sprinkle pepper over potatoes.

Mix soups, milk and garlic powder.

Pour this mixture over the potatoes.

Bake, uncovered, at 350 degrees for 45 minutes.

Color Me

Deviled Baked Potatoes

serves 4

4 baking potatoes
1 small can deviled ham
1 jar of your favorite cheese spread

Scrub potatoes.

Then bake at 450 degrees for 1 hour.

Cut a cross in each potato and top the steaming white inside
with several spoonfuls of deviled ham and a dab of your
favorite cheese sauce (blue cheese is especially good).

Nutty Turkey Stuffing

serves 6 to 8

1 package prepared dry stuffing
1/2 cup chopped Spanish peanuts
1/2 cup chopped celery

Prepare stuffing according to package directions.

Stir in peanuts and celery.

Place stuffing in turkey.

Vegetables

Corn Pudding

Some people think this pudding is better than chocolate!
serves 4

1 (1-pound) can cream-style corn
1 cup milk
1/4 teaspoon black pepper
4 slices white bread
1 slice cooked bacon, crumbled

Beat eggs with rotary beater.

•

Then add corn, milk, black pepper and bread
(which has been broken into small pieces).

•

Place bacon bits into greased casserole dish.

•

Pour in corn mixture. Bake at 350 degrees for 40 minutes.

Creole Green Beans

serves 4

1 (9-ounce) package frozen green beans,
cooked and drained
1 teaspoon minced onion
1/3 cup chili sauce
1/2 teaspoon marjoram

Mix in saucepan green beans, onion,
chili sauce and marjoram.

•

Cook only until thoroughly heated, stirring often.

Red, Green and Good

serves 6

2 (9-ounce) packages frozen French-style green beans
1/2 pint cherry tomatoes
2 tablespoons Italian dressing
1 teaspoon garlic powder

Cook green beans according to package directions.
•
Add tomatoes, dressing and garlic salt.
•
Heat through and serve.

Vegetable Mix

serves 6

1 (16-ounce) can French-style green beans, drained
1 (16-ounce) can bean sprouts, drained
2 (8-ounce) cans sliced mushrooms, drained
1/4 cup grated Parmesan cheese
1 (8-ounce) can tomato sauce
1 (3 1/2-ounce) can french fried onion rings

Toss together green beans, bean sprouts, mushrooms
and grated cheese.
•
Place in covered casserole dish.
•
Pour tomato sauce over vegetables.
•
Cover and bake at 350 degrees for 35 minutes.
•
Uncover dish and sprinkle with french fried
onion rings and bake 10 minutes longer.

Scalloped Onions and Tomatoes

serves 4

1 1/2 cups dry bread crumbs
1/4 cup margarine, melted
1 1/2 cups tomatoes (canned or fresh)
3 medium-size onions, sliced very thin
1/2 teaspoon oregano
1/8 teaspoon pepper

Add bread crumbs to the margarine and mix well.

•

In a well-greased baking dish, pour in just enough tomatoes
(about 1/2 cup) to cover the bottom.

•

Add a layer of bread-crumb mixture and cover with
a layer of onions. Sprinkle with oregano and pepper.

•

Then repeat layers, ending with bread crumbs on top.
Bake at 375 degrees for 40 minutes.

Quick-as-a-Wink Spinach

serves 6

2 (10-ounce) packages frozen spinach, cooked and drained
2 teaspoons minced onion
1/3 cup sour cream
1 tablespoon prepared horseradish
1/2 teaspoon salt

Combine all ingredients in a saucepan, and
cook over low heat until hot (about 5 minutes).

Magic-Six Tomatoes

Six is the magic number with these tomatoes!
serves 4

2 large tomatoes, cut in half
1 teaspoon sugar
Basil
Pepper
1/2 teaspoon garlic powder
4 thin slices of onion
2 tablespoons grated Parmesan cheese

For each tomato half do 6 things: sprinkle with
1/4 teaspoon sugar, dash of basil, dash of pepper,
1/8 teaspoon garlic powder, thin slice of onion
and 1/2 tablespoon grated cheese.

Bake in 500-degree oven for 5 minutes.

Take-on-a-Picnic Salad

serves 6

1 (18-ounce) bag frozen mixed vegetables, cooked
1/3 cup chopped onion
1 head lettuce, torn into bite-size pieces
2/3 cup mayonnaise

Drain vegetables and set in refrigerator to cool.

Toss cooled vegetables, onion and lettuce with
mayonnaise in large bowl and serve.

Santa Cruz Casserole

serves 4

1 (16-ounce) can tomatoes, drained
1 (12-ounce) can whole kernel corn
1/2 cup green pepper, chopped
1/4 cup onions, chopped
1/4 teaspoon pepper
2 tablespoons melted butter
1/4 cup seasoned bread crumbs
1/4 cup grated Parmesan cheese

Combine first 6 ingredients in a casserole dish.
•
Mix butter, bread crumbs and cheese and
sprinkle over top of casserole.
•
Bake 20 minutes in preheated 400-degree oven.

Milky Way Peas

serves 6

1/2 cup milk
2 (10-ounce) packages frozen peas
2 tablespoons butter
1/2 teaspoon honey

Heat milk.
•
Add frozen peas and stir until peas and milk are well mixed.
•
Cook over low heat for 5 minutes.
•
Stir in butter and honey and serve.

Desserts

Gooey Butterscotch Brownies

*Make these special brownies whenever you get
a chance. They are wonderful!
yield: 35*

2 cups (12-ounce) package butterscotch bits

1/2 cup brown sugar

1/2 cup margarine

2 eggs

1 1/2 cups flour

2 teaspoons baking powder

1/2 teaspoon salt

2 teaspoons vanilla

2 cups (12-ounce) package semisweet chocolate bits

2 cups miniature marshmallows

1 cup chopped pecans

In large saucepan melt butterscotch pieces, sugar and
margarine over medium heat, stirring constantly.

Remove from heat.

Sift flour, baking powder and salt together.
Add to egg mixture.

Finally, stir in vanilla, chocolate pieces,
marshmallows and pecans.

Spread in 10-by-15-inch greased pan.

Bake at 350 degrees for 20 to 25 minutes.

When cool, cut into bars.

Chocolate Mint Pudding

When "just chocolate" won't do.
serves 4

1 package chocolate pudding mix
5 (3-inch) peppermint sticks

Cook pudding according to package directions.

As mix cooks, drop 1 peppermint stick, broken into small pieces, into mix.

When pudding is thick, pour into 4 dishes and top each with a peppermint stick.

Red, White and Blue Sundae

serves 1

1 large scoop raspberry sherbet
1 small scoop vanilla ice cream
1/2 cup blueberries
1 tablespoon whipped cream
1 cherry

Place raspberry scoop on plate.

Top with slightly smaller scoop of vanilla ice cream.

Add blueberries, whipped cream and cherry.

Happy July 4th!

Chocolate Chip-Nut Pie

serves 8

1 cup sugar
1/2 cup flour
2 eggs, slightly beaten
1 stick butter or margarine, melted and cooled
1 cup English walnuts, broken
1 cup chocolate chips
1 teaspoon vanilla
1 unbaked pie shell

Mix sugar and flour.

Add eggs, melted butter, walnuts, chocolate chips and vanilla.

Pour into unbaked pie shell and bake in preheated
325-degree oven for 1 hour.

Test with toothpick before removing from oven to be sure
filling is not runny.

Strawberry Pie

serves 6

1 cooked pie shell
1 (3-ounce) package strawberry gelatin
1 cup boiling water
1 (10-ounce) box frozen strawberries

Melt gelatin in the boiling water. Then add frozen strawberries
and stir until ice dissolves. Let stand for 10 minutes, pour
into pie shell and chill 2 hours until firm.

Quick Indian Pudding

serves 4

2/3 cup Instant Cream of Wheat
2 1/2 cups milk
1/4 cup molasses
1/2 teaspoon cinnamon
1/4 cup sugar

Place cream of wheat, milk, molasses, cinnamon and sugar
in saucepan. Stir constantly over low heat until mixture
forms bubbles and let boil for 1/2 minute.

Remove from heat and pour into dessert dishes. Serve warm
with cream or vanilla ice cream.

Blizzard Cake

*This cake is lots of fun to decorate,
and you can do it by yourself.*
serves 10

1 package of white cake mix
1 can chocolate frosting
2 cups popped corn

Bake cake according to package instructions.

Cool.

Ice with chocolate frosting and cover entire cake with a
blizzard of popcorn snowflakes.

Peach Crumbly

serves 6

2 (#2) cans sliced peaches, drained
1 stick pie crust mix
1 (2 1/2-ounce) package slivered almonds
1 cup brown sugar
Butter

Place peaches in shallow baking dish.

•

Mix pie crust mix, nuts and sugar.

•

Sprinkle over peaches.

•

Dot generously with butter and bake at 325 degrees
for 30 minutes.

•

Serve with cream or vanilla ice cream.

Peanut Butter Pudding

serves 4

1 package vanilla instant pudding
1/4 cup crunchy peanut butter
4 tablespoons marshmallow topping

Prepare pudding as directed.

•

Beat in peanut butter with a rotary beater.

•

Spoon pudding into dessert dishes. Top with marshmallow
and chill in refrigerator for 1 hour.

All Kinds of Snowballs

*These are almost as much fun to make as real snowballs —
and taste better besides.*

**Vanilla ice cream
Coconut, flaked or shredded
Sauce (chocolate, caramel, butterscotch, strawberry
or pineapple)**

With an ice cream scoop, form balls of vanilla ice cream.

•

Roll in coconut.

•

Place on cookie sheet in freezer until firm.

•

Serve with favorite sauce.

Just Strawberries

serves 1

**1/8 cup brown sugar
1/8 cup sour cream (or yogurt)
1/2 dozen whole strawberries, with stems and leaves**

Put brown sugar and sour cream side by side in center of a
large dessert plate.

•

Surround by strawberries.

•

To eat, hold berry by stem and dip first in sour cream;
then in sugar.

As Easy as Eating Homemade Ice Cream

Once you make this ice cream, you'll be a hero to your family and friends. And there's no cooking.
serves 10

6 eggs
1 1/2 cups sugar
2 cartons half-and-half
3 1/2 pints whipping cream
Rock salt
Crushed ice

Beat eggs till foamy.

•

Add sugar and beat again for a minute.

•

Add half-and-half and cream.

•

Beat 2 minutes until well mixed.

•

Pour into ice cream container, cover tightly and place in freezer tub. Pack one-third of the freezer with ice and add layers of salt and ice around the container until the freezer is full.

•

For vanilla ice cream: add 3 tablespoons vanilla.

•

For chocolate: add 1 can Hershey's fudge topping.

•

(Mix flavorings in before freezing.)

Cookies

Circus Cookies

yield: 5 1/2 dozen

1 cup butter
1 1/2 cups brown sugar
3 cups sifted flour
1/2 teaspoon salt
1/2 teaspoon soda
2 eggs
2 teaspoons vanilla
2 cups peanuts
Sugar

Cream butter and brown sugar.
•
Sift flour, salt and soda together.
•
Add eggs, vanilla and sifted dry ingredients
to butter and sugar mixture.
•
Stir in peanuts.
•
Shape into balls about the size of a walnut. Place
about 2 inches apart on ungreased cookie sheet.
•
Flatten with a fork to about 1/3 inch.
Sprinkle with granulated sugar.
•
Bake in a 350-degree oven for 12 to 15 minutes.

Hopscotch Jumbles

yield: 2 1/2 dozen

1/2 cup peanut butter
1 (6-ounce) package butterscotch bits
1 (3-ounce) can chow mein noodles
1 cup miniature marshmallows

Melt peanut butter and butterscotch bits in double
boiler over hot water. Remove from heat.

Stir in noodles and marshmallows.

Drop by teaspoonfuls onto waxed paper. Chill until set.

Mexican Wedding Cake Cookies

yield: 4 dozen

1 cup butter
1/4 cup powdered sugar
1 teaspoon vanilla
2 cups sifted flour
1 cup chopped nuts

Beat butter and sugar until light.

Add vanilla and flour and mix well; stir in nuts.

Shape into balls and flatten to 1/4-inch thickness.

Bake in 325-degree oven for 20 minutes.

Roll in more powdered sugar while cookies are still hot.

Graham Cracker Sandwiches

These sandwiches are fun to make.
serves 1

1 thin slice of raw apple
2 graham crackers
1/4 of a flat chocolate bar
1 marshmallow

Put apple slice on a cracker, then chocolate and marshmallow.

•

Place on cookie sheet and place in 500-degree oven.
Watch carefully until marshmallow starts
to turn brown. Remove from oven.

•

Top with another graham cracker. Press down until the
marshmallow goes squish into the melted chocolate.

Hidden Treasure Cookies

It's what's inside that's good.
yield: 1 1/2 dozen

1 roll refrigerated sugar cookie dough
2 chocolate peanut bars

Cut cookie dough into 1/4-inch slices.

•

For each hidden cookie place piece of candy on a cookie
slice and top with another cookie.

•

Press edges together.

•

Bake on ungreased cookie sheet for 8 to 10 minutes.

Cornflake Cookies

yield: 3 dozen

1/2 cup butter
1/2 cup granulated sugar
1/2 cup brown sugar, firmly packed
1 egg
1 cup flour
1 1/2 teaspoons baking powder
1/4 teaspoon salt
1 cup shredded coconut
1 cup cornflakes

Cream butter with sugars.

•

Beat egg into mixture.

•

Sift flour, baking powder and salt and add to batter.

•

Stir in coconut and cornflakes.

•

Drop by level tablespoons 2 inches apart on
ungreased cookie sheet.

•

Bake in 350-degree oven for about 10 minutes.
Cool slightly before removing from cookie sheet.

Color Me

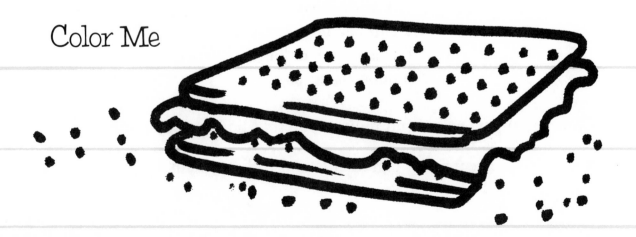

Somemores

This cookie has been a favorite of campers,
for many, many years.
serves 1

1 banana
2 squares sweet chocolate
1 caramel, cut in half
6 miniature marshmallows

Split banana so that you can fill it with the chocolate,
caramel and marshmallows. Then wrap banana in tin
foil and bake for 5 minutes at 400 degrees (or until
candies are melted).

Great dessert for a picnic!

No Bake Cookie Balls

yield: 4 dozen

2 cups sugar
1/4 cup cocoa
1/2 cup milk
1 stick butter
1/2 cup peanut butter
1 teaspoon vanilla
3 cups rolled oats

Combine sugar, cocoa and milk in pan and boil for one minute.

Add remaining ingredients and roll into balls.

Eat!

Gumdrop Cookies

Lots of stirring, rolling, squishing and eating!
yield: 4 dozen

1/2 cup butter
1/2 cup granulated sugar
1/2 cup brown sugar
2 eggs
1 cup, plus 2 tablespoons flour
1/2 teaspoon baking powder
1/2 teaspoon baking soda
1/4 teaspoon salt
1 cup spiced gumdrops, cut in small pieces
1 cup uncooked cornflakes
1/2 cup moist coconut

Cream butter and sugars and add eggs. Sift flour, baking
powder, soda and salt and add to butter and sugar mixture.
Stir in remaining ingredients. Chill in refrigerator.

•

Roll in round balls, about the size of walnuts

•

Place on cookie sheet and flatten slightly with a fork.

•

Bake in 350-degree oven until light brown,
but not hard, about 10 minutes.

Color Me

Skillet Cookies

yield: 3 dozen

1/3 cup butter
2 eggs
1 cup sugar
1 cup chopped dates
2 cups Rice Krispies
Coconut or finely chopped nuts

Melt butter in skillet.

●

Beat eggs until foamy; add sugar and stir well.
Pour into skillet.

●

Add chopped dates.

●

Cook about 15 minutes over very low heat,
stirring frequently as mixture bubbles.

●

Let stand until lukewarm. Stir in Rice Krispies.

●

Form into balls about the size of a walnut and roll
in coconut or chopped nuts.

●

Store in tight tin box.

Foods from Famous Friends

Mister Rogers' Snow Pudding

*Everyone on television's "Mister Rogers' Neighborhood"
loves "Snow Pudding." It tastes good but most of all it is fun to
prepare. Mr. Rogers describes how he makes snow you can eat:
"Presto! An egg white so clear you can see through it plops
into the mixing bowl and in just a minute an egg beater
whips it into a fluffy mountain." Add the other ingredients and
the fluffy mountain tastes different from any snow
that has ever melted in your mouth!*
serves 6 to 8

3/4 cup sugar
1 tablespoon unflavored gelatin (1 envelope)
1 1/4 cups lemon juice
1 tablespoon grated lemon rind
2 egg whites

Mix together sugar, gelatin and water in saucepan.

•

Stir constantly, while bringing to a boil.

•

Blend in lemon juice and rind.

•

Place pan in cold water and cool until mixture mounds
when dropped from a spoon.

•

Beat egg white until stiff.

•

Using rotary beater, slowly blend gelatin mixture
into beaten egg whites.

•

After blending, stir mixture with rubber spatula until it
holds its shape.

•

Spoon into dessert dishes or mold and chill until firm.

Captain Kangaroo's Banana Delight

Bob Keeshan, beloved by children as Captain Kangaroo, has many young friends who enjoy making his favorite recipe, "Banana Delight."

Graham Cracker Crust

Combine 2 cups graham cracker crumbs and 6 tablespoons melted butter.

Filling

1 cup butter
2 cups confectioner's sugar
3 eggs
1 teaspoon vanilla
4 or 5 large bananas — sliced — not combined with above

Cream butter. Add sugar gradually.
•
Add eggs, one at a time. Add vanilla.
•
Pat graham cracker crumbs into a 9-by-13-inch pan.
•
Pour filling in. Place bananas on top.

Topping

2 cups heavy cream
1/4 cup sugar
1 teaspoon vanilla

Beat all three ingredients until fluffy.
•
Put this "whipped cream" combination on top of bananas.
Refrigerate overnight.

Bill Cosby's Monkey Bread

*Bill Cosby's love for children led him to pursue and acquire a
doctorate in Education from the University of Massachusetts.
Monkey bread is a favorite of his, as prepared by his cook, Edith Bell.
With just a little supervision, you should manage this one quite well!*
yield: 1 loaf

5 cups flour
2 packages active dry yeast
1/3 cup sugar
1 teaspoon salt
1/2 cup water
1/2 cup milk
1/2 cup butter
3 large eggs
1 cup melted butter

Combine 1 1/2 cups flour, yeast, sugar and salt in a
large mixer bowl.

•

In a saucepan heat water, milk and butter until warm
(the butter need not melt) and add to flour mixture.

•

Add eggs and beat at low speed until moistened,
and at medium speed for 3 minutes.

•

Add remaining flour to make soft dough and knead
on a floured surface for 8 to 10 minutes.

•

Place in a greased bowl, turning to grease top.

Let rise in a warm place until light and doubled,
about 1 hour.

Punch down, turn out on floured board and
roll out 1/4 inch thick.

Cut dough into diamonds with a cookie cutter.

Dip each piece into the melted butter and
arrange in a buttered "monkey pan" (10-inch tube).

Cover and let rise again until almost doubled,
about 1 hour.

Bake at 375 degrees for 45 minutes
until browned and done.

Color Me

Clare Boothe Luce's French Toast

French toast was one of Clare Luce's favorite foods as a child. She writes, "It was my busy mother's favorite dish too because I could make it myself and so could my brother." In addition to breakfast, it can be served as a luncheon dish, sprinkled with brown or powdered sugar. And it also can be served as a dessert, with your favorite cookies, fruits or jam.
serves 1

1 egg
1/4 cup milk
1 teaspoon sugar
2 slices bread, with crusts removed

Beat egg well.
•
Stir in milk and sugar.
•
Soak the bread in the egg mixture for one minute.
•
Put one pat of butter in a frying pan, over low heat.
•
Just before butter turns brown, carefully lift bread from bowl,
place in pan and fry on both sides over medium heat
until bread is light golden brown.

Davy Crockett's Ham Biscuits

Here's a meal for someone as hungry as a "B'ar,"
and it's easy to fix, too. Pack up a bundle
for on the trail. Guaranteed to satisfy the
taste buds and appetite of any hunter.
serves 5 (or 1 hungry bear!)

1 (6 3/4-ounce) can ham, drained and flaked
1 teaspoon instant minced onion
1 teaspoon poppy seed
2 tablespoons butter, softened
2 teaspoons mustard
1 (10-ounce) can refrigerator biscuits
5 (4-by-4-inch) natural Swiss cheese slices

Combine first 5 ingredients and set aside about 1/3 cup.

●

Separate dough into 10 biscuits.

●

Press 5 biscuits into 3 1/2-inch circles on ungreased cookie sheet.

●

Spoon 1/4 cup meat mixture onto each flattened biscuit.

●

Fold cheese slices into quarters and press onto meat mixture.

●

Spoon remaining meat mixture over cheese.

●

Press remaining 5 biscuits into 4-inch circles and
slightly stretch each over meat mixture.

●

Do not seal edges.

●

Sprinkle tops with poppy seed.

●

Bake at 375 degrees for 10 to 15 minutes or until golden brown.

Popeye's Spinach Salad

serves 6

1 package fresh spinach
1 can bean sprouts, drained
8 slices crisp bacon, crumbled
3 hard-cooked eggs, diced
1 cup salad oil
1/2 cup sugar
1/3 cup catsup
1/4 cup red wine vinegar
1 tablespoon Worcestershire sauce

Tear spinach into bite-size pieces.

In large bowl, toss spinach, sprouts, bacon and eggs.

Combine last 5 ingredients in a small bowl.

Pour over salad ingredients and toss well.

Color Me

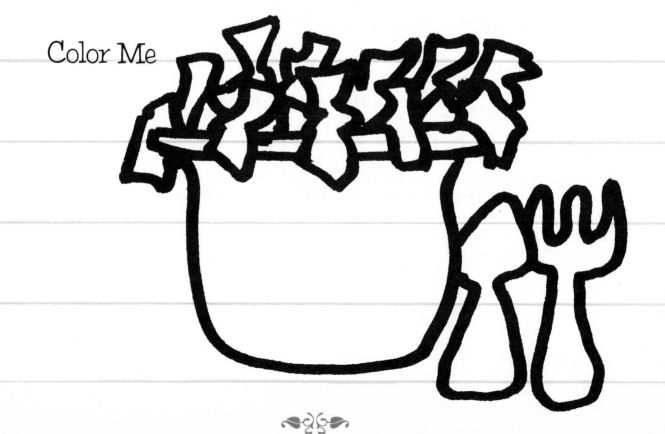

Mrs. Billy Graham's Tsao Fan: "Chinese Fried Rice, Ham and Eggs"

*Ruth Graham, the daughter of missionary parents,
grew up in China. One of the highlights of her childhood was the
yearly train ride to Shanghai. The best part of the trip was the
"Tsao Fan" served in the dining car: fried ham and
scrambled eggs, mixed with fried rice. Today, it is a favorite meal
of the Graham children. Mrs. Graham writes,
"Bowls and chopsticks are a must!"
serves 4*

2 cups cold cooked rice

2 tablespoons salad oil

2 to 3 slices ham

2 eggs, beaten

2 tablespoons soy sauce

Cook rice in oil over medium heat until golden colored,
stirring constantly.

●

Cut 2 slices of ham into small pieces and cook in butter
until golden.

●

Add to rice.

●

Finally, add beaten eggs to rice-ham mixture and stir over
medium heat until egg is set — about 10 seconds.

●

Instead of salt, sprinkle soy sauce over all, if desired.

Barbara Walters' Brownies

Barbara Walters' favorite dish as a child was her mother's stuffed cabbage but her own daughter Jacqueline's favorite is brownies. These special brownies keep well, if you don't eat them all in one or two sittings!
yield: 16

2 1/2 squares unsweetened chocolate
1/3 cup shortening
1 cup granulated sugar
2 eggs, well beaten
1/2 cup self-rising flour
1/2 cup chopped walnuts
1 teaspoon vanilla

Preheat oven to 375 degrees.
•
Melt chocolate and shortening together.
•
Add sugar to the well-beaten eggs.
•
Combine the mixtures.
•
Sift flour into the mixture.
•
Add nuts and vanilla. Blend.
•
Spread the dough evenly in a greased square
8-by-8-by-2-inch pan.
•
Bake for 20 to 25 minutes.
•
When cool, cut into squares or bars.

Julie Andrews' Oatmeal Cookies

*What does the fabulous Mary Poppins eat when she is
hungry for a snack? Oatmeal cookies have been
Julie Andrews' favorites for a long time. Today she
bakes them often for her children and their friends.
An added bonus is that the cookies are, in her words, "very healthy."
yield: 2 dozen*

2 sticks butter, melted
1/2 cup brown sugar, packed in cup
4 tablespoons molasses
5 cups quick-cooking rolled oats

Mix melted butter with the brown sugar and molasses.

Add the oats and mix. If too moist, add more oats.

Press into a greased 9-by-13-inch baking pan and bake at
350 degrees 15 to 20 minutes.

Cut in pan before cooling.

Color Me

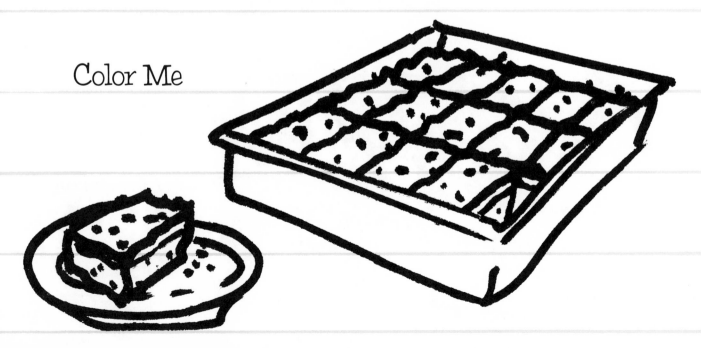

Big Bird's Honey Bananas

*Yummy alone or with eggs or anything, Big Bird whips
these up in his nest kitchen in no time at all!*
serves 2

2 bananas
Honey
Butter

Melt a little butter in a frying pan.

•

Slice the two bananas in half lengthwise.

•

Place them in the pan, flat-side down.

•

Pour a strip of honey on the top side of each half.

•

Cook just one minute on each side.

Color Me

My Favorite Recipe

Index